Beginner's English Reader

High-interest stories for building communication skills

Barbara Dogger

Illustrations by Phil Kantz

National Textbook Company
a division of NTC/CONTEMPORARY PUBLISHING GROUP
Lincolnwood, Illinois USA

Preface

Beginner's English Reader is a delightful book designed to make English enjoyable for junior high school through adult students at the beginning level. Through 27 lively, self-contained vignettes, students are introduced to and follow the adventures of likeable and engaging characters. Culturally authentic and often amusing scenes are portrayed through dialogue, and students will enjoy seeing how various friends, families, neighbors, and other community members interact with each other.

The language employed in *Beginner's English Reader* is simplified, but authentic. The exclusive use of the present tense, and the avoidance of subordinate clauses make this a manageable reader that beginning students will be able to handle successfully. The vocabulary chosen for the stories, which can be read in any sequence, is of high frequency, and words are repeated often to encourage mastery.

Each of the readings is followed by one or more exercises, including reading comprehension, vocabulary reinforcement, and free completion. A few word puzzles are included for motivation and enjoyment.

Contents

1 The Johnson Family

In the U.S.A.,

there is a city.

In the city there is an apartment house.

In the apartment house there is an apartment.

In the apartment there is a living room.

In the living room we find the Johnson family. The parents are Mr. and Mrs. Johnson. The children are called Tim and Linda. The dog's name is Flash.

A Answer the questions.

1 What is in the U.S.A.?
2 What is in the city?
3 What is in the apartment house?
4 What is in the apartment?
5 What are the parents' names?
6 What are the children's names?
7 What is the dog's name?

B Write these words.

1 a city   2 an apartment   3 a living room

4 a dog   5 a family

2 In the Morning

At 7:00 A.M. Mr. Johnson goes to the railroad station. He carries a lunchbox. In the lunchbox there is a sandwich, potato chips, and an apple.

At 7:15 A.M. Mrs. Johnson goes to the post office. She works at the post office in the mornings. She is carrying a tote bag. A sweater is in the tote bag.

At 7:45 A.M. Linda and Tim go to school. They are carrying books and notebooks.

Flash stays at home. He is looking at the door. He is sad.

A Answer the questions.
1 Where is Mr. Johnson going?
2 What is he carrying?
3 What is in his lunchbox?
4 Where is Mrs. Johnson going?
5 When does she work at the post office?
6 What is in her tote bag?
7 Where are Linda and Tim going?
8 What are they carrying?
9 Who remains in the apartment?
10 How does Flash feel?

B Write the words.
1 railroad station
2 sandwich
3 apple
4 potato chips
5 post office
6 tote bag
7 school
8 notebook
9 book

3 At Grandma Smith's House

Tim and his friend, Bob, are buying bread, milk, bananas, and oranges at the supermarket. Then they go to Grandma Smith's house. It is snowing.

Grandma Smith is sitting in an easy chair. She is 80 years old, and today she is staying in her apartment.

Bob places the bread, milk, bananas, and oranges on the table. Grandma Smith gives the boys a piece of cake. "Thank you," she says. "This is very nice."

Mimi, the cat, sees the milk and climbs onto the table.
She says, "Meow."

A Answer the questions.
1 What are Tim and Bob buying at the supermarket?
2 Where do they go after that?
3 How is the weather?
4 Where is Grandma Smith sitting?
5 How old is she?
6 Where is Grandma Smith staying today?
7 Where does Bob place the food?
8 What does Grandma Smith give the boys?
9 What does she say?
10 Who gets up on the table?

B Write the words.
1 supermarket
2 bread
3 milk
4 bananas
5 oranges
6 apartment
7 easy chair

4 Scott's Dog

It is Wednesday at seven o'clock in the evening. Linda and Tim are playing table tennis with Amy and Scott. They are playing in the garage.

Linda is playing with Scott. He is very nice and plays well. Tim is playing with Amy. She is also very nice, but she plays quite badly.

Scott's dog comes into the garage, and he runs away with the ball.

"Wow!" says Linda. But Tim is not angry. The game is over.

A Answer the questions.
1 What day is it?
2 How late is it?
3 Where are Linda and Tim playing?
4 Does Scott play well?
5 Is Amy nice?
6 How does she play?
7 Who runs away with the ball?
8 What does Linda say?
9 Who is not angry?
10 What is finished?

B Complete the sentences.
1 Linda and Scott are playing _____ .
2 Amy plays _____ .
3 Scott's dog runs away with _____ .
4 Tim is _____ .

Mrs. Johnson Cake with whipped cream please, sir.
Waiter Certainly, ma'am.
Man Waiter! Waiter! A cup of coffee!
Waiter Of course, sir.
Young girl A chocolate ice cream, please.
Waiter Yes, of course.
Students Three colas and some water, please.
Man Hurry up, waiter. I'm thirsty.
Waiter Yes, sir. I'm coming. Here is your chocolate ice cream.
Man Please! Please! Where is my coffee?

A Answer the questions.
1 Where is Mrs. Johnson?
2 What does she order?
3 What does the man order?
4 What does the young girl order?
5 What do the students order?
6 Who tells the waiter to hurry up?

B Write the words.
1 a coffee shop
2 cake with whipped cream
3 a cup of coffee
4 a chocolate ice cream
5 a cola
6 a waiter
7 a student

6 In the Yard

It is noontime. Tim and his friends are playing ball in front of the apartment. In front of Grandma Smith's apartment there are flowers.

Grandma Smith and the apartment manager are also in front of the apartment. They are speaking together. Tim kicks the ball. The ball hits and breaks a flowerpot.

"I'm sorry, Grandma Smith!" Tim says.

"Oh, it's not so bad, Tim," Grandma Smith answers.

The apartment manager thinks otherwise. He doesn't like Tim.

"I'm going to tell your father!" he yells.

Tim is worried. His father is in bed. He is sleeping.

A Answer the questions.

1 What time is it?

2 Who is playing ball with his friends?

3 Where are some flowers?

4 Where are Grandma Smith and the apartment manager?

5 What does Tim break with the ball?

6 What does he say to Grandma Smith?

7 What does she answer?

8 What does the apartment manager yell?

9 Who is worried?

10 Where is Mr. Johnson?

B Complete the sentences.

1 Tim and his friends are playing ball _____ .

2 There are _____ in front of Grandma Smith's apartment.

3 When Tim breaks the flowerpot, Grandma Smith says, "_____ ."

4 The apartment manager _____ at Tim.

15

7 The Rock Concert

It is Saturday night. Tim and Linda are at the rock concert in the park. They are sitting on the grass.

The star on stage is singing loudly. His name is Michael. The girls in the audience are screaming. Linda is, too.

A young man near Linda asks her, "Do you want to dance with me?" He laughs and gives her a cola.

"Watch out!" Tim says to him. "My sister can only see the star on stage. You haven't got a chance."

"Be quiet!" Linda screams. "Isn't he wonderful?"

A Answer the questions.

1 What night is it?
2 Where are Tim and Linda?
3 Where are they sitting?
4 What is the star doing on stage?
5 What are the girls in the audience doing?
6 What does the young man ask Linda?
7 Who is the only person that Linda sees?
8 What does she scream?

B Complete the sentences.

1 The star sings _____ .
2 Near Linda sits _____ .
3 He wants her to _____ .
4 Linda screams, "_____ ."

8 How Are You Doing?

Linda is in the basement. Here we find an old bed, an easy chair, a metal closet, and a suitcase. Linda goes over to the closet. She opens it and finds a dictionary.

Suddenly it is dark. The book falls on the floor. Linda tries to go to the door and she bumps against the bed. "Ow!" she cries.

Then it is bright in the basement again. Her brother stands in the doorway and smiles.

"How are you doing?" he asks. Linda throws a pillow at Tim's head.

"How are you doing?" she asks. Tim doesn't answer. He is already running up the stairs.

A Answer the questions.
1 Where is Linda?
2 What is in the basement?
3 What does Linda find in the closet?
4 What happens suddenly?
5 What falls on the floor?
6 Where does Linda want to go?
7 Who is standing in the doorway?
8 What does she throw at Tim's head?
9 What does she ask him?
10 Where is Tim already?

B Complete the sentences.
1 In the basement there are _____ .
2 It is dark and a book _____ .
3 Then the basement _____ again.
4 Linda _____ at Tim's head.

9 Watching TV

Tim, Linda, and Mr. Johnson are sitting in front of the
TV. They see a man. He is crossing the street and he is
carrying a suitcase.

"Linda!" Mrs. Johnson calls from the kitchen.

On the screen two policemen appear. The man runs
across a bridge. A train is approaching.

"Linda! Linda!" Mrs. Johnson calls again.

Suddenly, the man
springs onto the roof
of the train.

Mrs. Johnson comes into the living room. She sees a man on the train. The suitcase falls from the roof of the train. Now Mrs. Johnson is sitting in front of the TV.

A Answer the questions.
1 Who is sitting in front of the TV?
2 Whom do they see?
3 What is he doing?
4 To whom does Mrs. Johnson speak?
5 Where is the man running?
6 Where does he jump suddenly?
7 Who comes into the living room?
8 Who does she see?
9 What falls from the roof of the train?
10 Now who is also sitting in front of the TV set?

B Complete the sentences.
1 Tim, Linda, and Mr. Johnson are sitting _____ .
2 When two policemen appear, the man on the screen

_____ .
3 Mrs. Johnson first calls, "_____ !"
4 Then she _____ .

21

10 A Volleyball Game

Linda and Tim go to the John F. Kennedy High School.
Today the volleyball team is playing against Washington
High School. Linda and her friend, Sue, are on the team.
They wear white T-shirts and blue shorts. Until now the
game is a tie. Each team has fourteen points. Sue hits the
ball to Linda. Linda hits the ball over the net. The
audience cheers.

Sue hits the ball to Linda again. Her friends cry, "Go, Linda, go!" Linda waits only a second. Then she hits the ball over the net.

"Go!" the audience cries. The referee blows the whistle. The game is over.

"Terrific, Linda!" Bob yells.

"Not bad!" yells Tim.

A Answer the questions.

1 What is the name of Tim and Linda's school?
2 Against whom is their volleyball team playing?
3 What are Linda and Sue wearing as members of the team?
4 How is the game going until now?
5 To whom does Sue hit the ball?
6 What do Linda's friends shout?
7 What does Linda do with the ball?
8 What does the referee do?
9 What does Bob say?
10 What does Tim say?

B Complete the sentences.

1 The two teams come from _____ High School and _____ High School.
2 When the game is a tie, each team has _____ points.
3 When the referee blows the whistle, the game _____ .
4 The team from _____ High School won the game.

11 On the Bench

Tim and Flash are sitting with Elaine on a bench.

Tim Do you want some ice cream, Elaine?

Elaine Oh yes! I love ice cream!

Tim Two chocolate ice cream cones, please.

Elaine Thank you, Tim.

Scott comes by.

Scott There you are, Elaine. I'm going to a movie. Do you want to come along?

Elaine Sure! So long, Tim and Flash.

Elaine and Scott walk off.

Tim Women! I'll never understand what they want!

A Answer the questions.

1 Who is sitting on the bench?
2 What does Tim ask?
3 Does Elaine like ice cream?
4 What does Tim do next?

5 Who comes walking by?
6 What does he ask Elaine?
7 What does she say?
8 How does Tim feel?

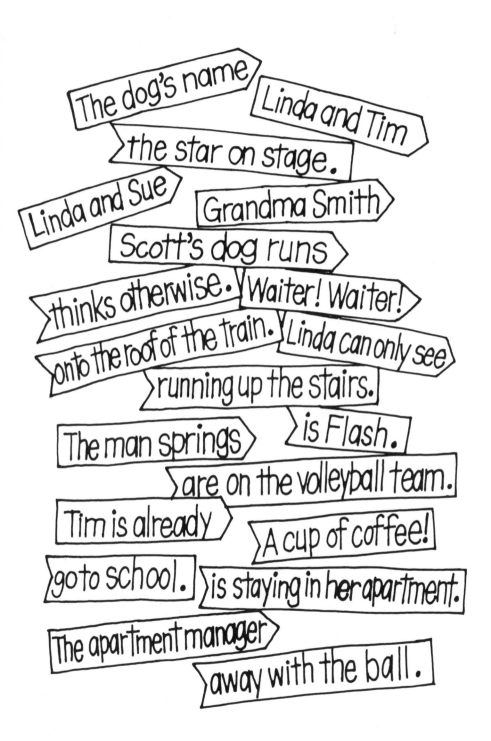

The dog's name

Linda and Tim

the star on stage.

Linda and Sue

Grandma Smith

Scott's dog runs

thinks otherwise.

Waiter! Waiter!

onto the roof of the train.

Linda can only see

running up the stairs.

The man springs

is Flash.

are on the volleyball team.

Tim is already

A cup of coffee!

go to school.

is staying in her apartment.

The apartment manager

away with the ball.

13 Tim's Slip of Paper

It is six o'clock in the evening. Tim is writing on a small slip of paper to his friend, Bob. Then he leaves the house.

Linda looks out of the window. Her brother is sticking his piece of paper in a can. Then he walks into the street.

He places the can near a tree. Five minutes later Linda goes with her friend, Mary, into the street. They read Tim's paper.

"Wow!" says Linda. "It's all in code!"

20, 8, 5   16, 1, 18, 20, 25
19, 20, 1, 18, 20, 19
1, 20   19, 5, 22, 5, 14

A Answer the questions.
1 What time is it?
2 What is Tim doing?
3 When Tim leaves the house, who is looking out of the window?
4 What does she see?
5 Five minutes later, what do Linda and Mary do?
6 What does Linda say?

B Follow the directions.
1 Read Tim's note.
2 Linda also writes a note. It is found below. Take a small mirror and read the note backwards.
3 Now write your own note. Use the "backward code" or another code that you create.

MEET ME AT THE PARK
AT FIVE

14 On a Motorcycle

Hank has a great motorcycle.

He asks Linda, "Do you want to ride with me on my motorcycle?"

"Oh! Yes!" says Linda. They ride very fast, and she likes that.

"Faster, Hank!" Linda shouts.

Hank goes 30, then 40 miles per hour.

Suddenly, they see a woman. She is crossing the street.

Hank brakes sharply, and he stops just in time.

He is pale, and Linda is, too.

"Are you crazy?" screams the woman.

A Answer the questions.
1 What does Hank have?
2 What does he ask Linda?
3 How are they traveling?
4 What does Linda shout?
5 How fast is Hank going?
6 Whom do they suddenly see?
7 What is the woman doing?
8 What does Hank do quickly?
9 How do Hank and Linda look and feel?
10 What does the woman say?

B Compare the measurements.
1 kilometer = ⅝ of a mile
100 kilometers = ⅝ × 100 = 500 eighths = 62½ miles

C How many miles does each of the figures below equal?
40 kilometers = _____
110 kilometers = _____
120 kilometers = _____

15 In Class

It is 10:15 A.M. Everyone is taking a math test. Linda is sitting near Susan, and she is whispering something.

"Quiet!" the teacher, Ms. Jones, says. She looks at the class.

Bill raises his hand. "I have a problem," he says. He must leave the class. Linda giggles.

Two minutes later he comes back. He sits at his desk in front of Linda, and he has something in his hand.

"Give me that slip of paper!" says Ms. Jones. "You are a cheat! Your father is going to hear about this."

"That is my biggest problem," says Bill. Then he leaves the class. Everyone laughs except for Ms. Jones.

A Answer the questions.

1 What time is it?
2 What is everyone doing?
3 What is Linda doing?
4 What does Ms. Jones say?
5 What does Bill do?
6 What must he do?
7 When he returns, what does Bill have in his hand?
8 What does Ms. Jones say now?
9 What does Bill say to this?
10 How do Ms. Jones and the class respond to this?

B Which word does not fit? Circle it.

1 school, post office, note, museum
2 giggle, laugh, whisper, study
3 Saturday, Wednesday, pretty, Monday

16 At the Open-air Market

Tim's uncle sells fruits and vegetables at an open-air market. Today is Wednesday. Tim is helping his uncle. He is opening up a box while Uncle John is selling a pound of cherries to a woman.

"Yes. They are very good today, ma'am," he says.

A young boy takes two peaches, sticks them in his pocket, and runs down the street.

Tim runs after him.
"Stop! Thief!" he cries.
A policeman sees both
of them.

The young boy stops.
Quickly he gives the
peaches back to Tim...

... and disappears.

A Answer the questions.
1 What does Tim's uncle do?
2 What day is today?
3 What is Tim doing?
4 What is Uncle John selling to the woman?
5 What does he say to her?
6 What does a young boy take?
7 What does Tim do?
8 What does he shout?
9 Who sees both of them?
10 What does the young boy do?

B Complete the sentences.
1 Uncle John sells _____ .
2 A young boy takes _____, sticks _____, and runs _____ .
3 Tim cries, "_____ !"
4 When the policeman arrives, the boy _____ .

33

17 After the Movie

It is Saturday at ten o'clock in the evening. Linda, Tim, and their friend, Bill, are leaving the movie theater. They walk by a small store.

"Look over there. The door is open," says Linda.

They walk inside. It is dark. Bill takes out his flashlight. On the counter in front of them, there is a bottle and two glasses. Nearby, there are a pair of watches, a ring, and a bracelet. Tim opens a cabinet.

Suddenly, a man appears behind the counter. He is wearing a hat and dark glasses. Linda screams.

"What are you doing here?" the man asks. His voice is hoarse. The three do not answer. They run out of the store. "Just like in the movies!" Linda says to herself.

A Answer the questions.
1 What time is it on Saturday?
2 What are Linda, Tim, and Bill leaving?
3 Where do they walk?
4 What do they notice?
5 What do they do?
6 What does Bill do next?
7 What is on the counter?
8 What is lying nearby?
9 Who appears suddenly behind the counter?
10 What is he wearing?
11 What does he ask?
12 What do the three do?

B Complete the sentences.
1 When Linda, Tim, and Bill notice that the door is open, they _____ .
2 Bill takes out his _____ .
3 When the man appears behind the counter, Linda

_____ .

4 When he speaks, they _____ .

18 The Fire

It is 7:00 P.M. Tim and Linda are in the kitchen. She is making a salad. Linda looks out the window. Flames are shooting up from the factory across the street.

"Tim, it's a fire!" screams Linda. The two run to the drugstore on the corner.

Tim runs faster than his sister. In the drugstore he phones the fire station.

The fire fighters come quickly and put out the fire. The next day there is a photograph of Tim in the newspaper. He is very happy.

A Copy the sentences and replace the incorrect words.

1 Tim and Linda are at school.
2 They are eating a salad.
3 Linda is looking in a cupboard.
4 "That's chewing gum!" she screams.
5 They run to the chemistry laboratory.
6 In the drugstore, Tim works for the fire fighters.
7 The fire fighters look for the fire.
8 In the newspaper there is a photograph of Tim and Linda on a motorcycle.

B Complete the sentences.

1 Tim and Linda see the fire at _____ P.M.
2 The flames are _____ .
3 They run to _____ on the corner.
4 There, Tim _____ the fire station.
5 When his photograph is in the newspaper, Tim is

_____ .

19 At the Railroad Station

Woman Where does the train from New York City arrive?

Mr. Johnson Track 12, ma'am.

Woman Thank you.

Man Where is the luggage counter, please?

Mr. Johnson Over there, sir.

Young woman Where is the restaurant?

Mr. Johnson Near Track 7.

Young boy Where are the restrooms?

Mr. Johnson Near the luggage counter.

Young girl Mama! Mama!

Mr. Johnson All these questions! Can't anyone read?

A Answer the questions.

1 Where does the train from New York City arrive?

2 Where is the restaurant?

3 Where are the restrooms?

4 What does Mr. Johnson say about all of these questions?

B Read the schedule and answer the questions.

From New York City

Departure	Train	Arrival	Destination
2:40 A.M.	#426	3:50 A.M.	Albany
6:41 A.M.	#122	7:50 A.M.	Baltimore
7:05 A.M.	#547	8:50 A.M.	Boston
7:29 A.M.	#816	10:17 A.M.	Buffalo
8:31 A.M.	#522	12:12 P.M.	Cleveland
9:20 A.M.	#916	10:50 A.M.	New Haven
10:37 A.M.	#526	12:05 P.M.	Philadelphia
11:17 A.M.	#124	1:24 P.M.	Pittsburgh
12:10 P.M.	#874	1:36 P.M.	Providence
12:35 P.M.	#624	1:40 P.M.	Schenectady
12:55 P.M.	#568	2:05 P.M.	Washington, D.C.

1 When does #426 leave New York City?

2 Where is it going?

3 How long does it take #547 to travel to Boston?

4 When does #874 depart for Providence?

5 When does #522 arrive in Cleveland?

6 How long does it take #522 to travel from New York City to Cleveland?

7 When does #124 leave New York City for Pittsburgh?

8 How long does it take #568 to travel from New York City to Washington, D.C.?

20 A Mishap

It is Thursday. Tim is riding his bike to school. A woman is walking with her dog. Suddenly, the dog runs directly in front of Tim after a cat. Tim falls from his bike.

"Ouch!" he cries.

Bob and Susan are also going to school. They see Tim, and they quickly run over to him.

"Are you hurt?" they ask.

"My pants and jacket are dirty," he answers.

The woman crosses the street and takes her dog in her arms. She doesn't even see Tim.

"Come, my precious," she says to the dog. Then she disappears.

A Answer the questions.

1 What day is it?
2 Where is Tim going on his bicycle?
3 Who is walking a dog?
4 Whom does the dog run after?
5 Why does Tim fall off his bike?
6 Who is also going to school?
7 When they see Tim, what do they do?
8 Is Tim hurt?
9 What does the woman do?
10 What does she say to her dog?

B Complete the sentences to describe the pictures.

Mrs. Johnson falls
from _____ .

Mr. Johnson falls
from _____ .

Tim falls from

_____ .

Elaine falls from

_____ .

21 A Language Problem

It is Sunday, and it is raining. Tim is going with his friends to the museum. They see old books, an old printing press, and other inventions.

"Very interesting," Bob says.

At 5:00 P.M. the museum closes. They all find themselves outside again, and a pretty girl comes up to them. She has an umbrella in her hand.

"Can you tell me where the museum is, please?" she asks Tim in French.

"Excuse me, Miss," he says. "I don't understand."

"Do you speak English? We don't speak French," explains Bob.

The girl shakes her head.

"It's a shame," says Tim. "Why don't we all speak the same language?"

A Answer the questions.

1 Where are Tim and his friends going?
2 What do they see in the museum?
3 When do they leave the museum?
4 Who walks up to them?
5 What does she have in her hand?
6 What information is she asking for?
7 What does Tim say to her?
8 What does Bob explain?
9 What does the girl do?
10 What does Tim say?

B Complete the sentences.

1 At the museum Tim and his friends see _____ .
2 A pretty girl comes up to them as they _____ .
3 She speaks _____ ; she doesn't speak _____ .
4 The boys wish that all people spoke _____ .

22 At the Wharf

It is eight o'clock in the morning. Linda and Tim are on their way to school. They run into Margery.

"It's a nice day, isn't it?" she asks. "I'm not going to school. I'm going to the harbor."

"So long," says Linda to her brother. "I'm going with Margery." A pair of boats are in the harbor. A friendly fisherman shows Linda a big fish.

"No thank you, sir," she says and smiles. The fisherman shows the girls a very nice café near the harbor. "Here they serve very good coffee and rolls," he says.

On the terrace of the café sits a man. He looks at them.
"Oh, my gosh!" says Linda. "That's my father!"

A Answer the questions.
1 What time is it?
2 Where are Tim and Linda going?
3 Whom do they meet?
4 Where is she going?
5 What does Linda say to Tim?
6 Why does the fisherman show Linda the big fish?
7 What does she say?
8 Where does the fisherman recommend that they eat?
9 Who is sitting on the terrace of the café?

B Complete the sentences.
1 It's a nice day, so Margery decides to go to _____ .
2 Linda decides to go _____ .
3 Linda _____ buy a fish from the fisherman.
4 Both Linda and Margery should be _____ .

23 In the Garden

Linda and Susan are in a garden. The garden is behind an old house. Susan is observing the goldfish in a small pond. Meanwhile, Linda climbs up into a tree.

Suddenly, a branch breaks and Linda falls into the pond.

"Ouch!" she cries.

"Is everything okay?" asks Susan.

Linda laughs.

"Everything is okay with me, but not with the goldfish."

A Answer the questions.

1 Where are Linda and Susan?
2 What is Susan doing?
3 What is Linda doing?
4 What happens next?
5 Is Linda hurt?
6 What is she concerned about?

B Complete the sentences.

1 The garden is located _____ .
2 Susan is observing _____ .
3 Linda _____ a tree.
4 When Linda falls into the pond, she worries about

_____ .

24 A Bike Tour

During a summer vacation, Tim, Linda, and their friends are going on a long bike trip. Each one has a backpack on his or her luggage rack. The weather is great!

At noon they take a break. In an hour they will travel down a river on a big wooden raft. Everybody is singing and having a good time.

The afternoon is hot. They go into a cool forest and they have their first picnic.

In the evening they arrive at their goal—a youth hostel at the base of the Adirondak Mountains. Everybody is tired. They all sleep well.

A Answer the questions.
1 What time of year is it?
2 Where are Tim, Linda, and their friends going?
3 Where does each person carry a backpack?
4 When do they stop for a break?
5 An hour later, what are they doing?
6 Where do they go for their first picnic?
7 Where do they arrive in the evening?
8 How does everyone feel?

B Complete the sentences.
1 Tim, Linda, and their friends take _____ during summer vacation.
2 As they travel down the river, everyone _____ .
3 Because the afternoon is hot, they eat their picnic _____ .

4 Because they are tired at the end of the day, they _____ .

25 At the Fountain

The next morning they travel to Geneva, New York. A couple of them stroll through this small town. There is a lot of traffic on the street. A small bus with tourists stops at the town square.

Linda and Hank are sitting near the fountain. An ice cream vendor comes along.

"Where is the lake?" asks Hank.

"It's right behind you," the ice cream vendor says. "Would you like some ice cream?"

"Good idea," says Linda.

"Two ice creams," orders Hank. He pays the vendor the money.

"Look over there," says Linda. "There is a man wearing high fishing boots. What is he doing?"

Hank answers, "He is going down to Seneca Lake to catch some fish for supper."

"Sounds like fun!" exclaims Linda.

A Answer the questions.

1 Where do they travel the next morning?
2 Where does the small bus with tourists stop?
3 Where are Linda and Hank sitting?
4 Who comes along?
5 What does Hank order?
6 What is right behind Linda and Hank?
7 What is the man wearing?
8 What is he planning to do?

B Write the words.

1 stroll
2 traffic
3 tourists
4 town square
5 ice cream vendor
6 high fishing boots
7 supper

On Sunday they all wander through the woods. Margery suddenly says, "Do you see the park ranger's tower overhead? We can see all of the animals in the park from up there."

So they all rush to the tower. They climb up the ladder. They can see one tree after another there, but no animals.

"Where is Linda?" asks Tim. She's not with them anymore. They are all frightened.

Finally they see her again. She is sitting behind a bush. "There's a deer," she says.

The others can only see a tail; then it's gone. "The ranger's tower wasn't a good idea," says Tim.

A Answer the questions.
1 What is everyone doing on Sunday?
2 What does Margery say?
3 What does everyone do?
4 What do they see?
5 What does Tim notice?
6 Where do they find Linda?
7 Why does Tim say that the ranger's tower was not a good idea?

B Complete the sentences.
1 Margery says that they can see a lot of _____ from the ranger's tower.
2 When they climb the tower, they see _____ .
3 Linda is sitting _____ .
4 She sees _____ ; the others only see _____ .

53

27 Niagara Falls

Summer vacation ends at Niagara Falls. It's a wonderful day, and they are all in a good mood.

They are all standing next to the falls. The sun is shining brightly on the water as it plunges to the depths below.

Everyone is talking excitedly. Tim exclaims, "Wow! Look at all that water! I would hate to fall over the edge!"

"Be quiet!" says Linda. "Listen to the sound of the falls."

Everyone stops to listen to this amazing sound from nature. They stand quietly for a while. Then they move on to get on the bus.

As they leave, Hank asks, "Wouldn't it be wonderful to listen to a rock concert here? What an echo!"

A Answer the questions.
1 Where does summer vacation end?
2 What kind of a day is it?
3 How do they feel?
4 What does Tim say?
5 What does Linda answer?
6 When they quit talking, what do they hear?
7 Where do they go when they leave the falls?
8 What does Hank say as they leave?

B Write the words.
1 summer vacation
2 Niagara Falls
3 shining
4 plunges
5 depths
6 nature
7 rock concert
8 echo